IPHIGENIA IN TAURIS

EURIPIDES

ISBN: 978-1502981189

CHARACTERS OF THE PLAY

IPHIGENIA, eldest daughter of Agamemnon, King of Argos; supposed to have been sacrificed by him to Artemis at Aulis.

ORESTES, her brother; pursued by Furies for killing his mother, Clytemnestra, who had murdered Agamemnon.

PYLADES, Prince of Phocis, friend to Orestes.

THOAS, King of Tauris, a savage country beyond the Symplegades.

A HERDSMAN.

A MESSENGER.

CHORUS of Captive Greek Women, handmaids to Iphigenia.

The Goddess PALLAS ATHENA.

[The Scene shows a great and barbaric Temple on a desolate sea-coast. An altar is visible stained with blood. There are spoils of slain men hanging from the roof. IPHIGENIA, in the dress of a Priestess, comes out from the Temple.]

IPHIGENIA.

Child of the man of torment and of pride
Tantalid Pelops bore a royal bride
On flying steeds from Pisa. Thence did spring
Atreus: from Atreus, linked king with king,
Menelaus, Agamemnon. His am I
And Clytemnestra's child: whom cruelly
At Aulis, where the strait of shifting blue
Frets with quick winds, for Helen's sake he slew,
Or thinks to have slain; such sacrifice he swore
To Artemis on that deep-bosomed shore.
  For there Lord Agamemnon, hot with joy
To win for Greece the crown of conquered Troy,
For Menelaus' sake through all distress
Pursuing Helen's vanished loveliness,
Gathered his thousand ships from every coast
Of Hellas: when there fell on that great host
Storms and despair of sailing. Then the King
Sought signs of fire, and Calchas answering

Spake thus: "O Lord of Hellas, from this shore
No ship of thine may move for evermore,
Till Artemis receive in gift of blood
Thy child, Iphigenia. Long hath stood
Thy vow, to pay to Her that bringeth light
Whatever birth most fair by day or night
The year should bring. That year thy queen did bear
A child—whom here I name of all most fair.
See that she die."

            So from my mother's side
By lies Odysseus won me, to be bride
In Aulis to Achilles. When I came,
They took me and above the altar flame

5

Held, and the sword was swinging to the gash,
When, lo, out of their vision in a flash
Artemis rapt me, leaving in my place
A deer to bleed; and on through a great space
Of shining sky upbore and in this town
Of Tauris the Unfriended set me down;
Where o'er a savage people savagely
King Thoas rules. This is her sanctuary
And I her priestess. Therefore, by the rite
Of worship here, wherein she hath delight—
Though fair in naught but name. ... But Artemis
Is near; I speak no further. Mine it is
To consecrate and touch the victim's hair;
Doings of blood unspoken are the care
Of others, where her inmost chambers lie.
Ah me!
But what dark dreams, thou clear and morning sky,
I have to tell thee, can that bring them ease!
Meseemed in sleep, far over distant seas,
I lay in Argos, and about me slept
My maids: and, lo, the level earth was swept
With quaking like the sea. Out, out I fled,
And, turning, saw the cornice overhead
Reel, and the beams and mighty door-trees down
In blocks of ruin round me overthrown.
One single oaken pillar, so I dreamed,
Stood of my father's house; and hair, meseemed,
Waved from its head all brown: and suddenly
A human voice it had, and spoke. And I,
Fulfilling this mine office, built on blood
Of unknown men, before that pillar stood,
And washed him clean for death, mine eyes astream
With weeping.

    And this way I read my dream.
Orestes is no more: on him did fall
My cleansing drops.—The pillar of the hall
Must be the man first-born; and they, on whom
My cleansing falls, their way is to the tomb.

Therefore to my dead brother will I pour
Such sacrifice, I on this bitter shore
And he beyond great seas, as still I may,
With all those maids whom Thoas bore away
In war from Greece and gave me for mine own.
But wherefore come they not? I must be gone
And wait them in the temple, where I dwell.

[She goes into the Temple.]

VOICE.
Did some one cross the pathway? Guard thee well.

ANOTHER VOICE.
I am watching. Every side I turn mine eye.

(Enter ORESTES and PYLADES. Their dress shows fhey are
travellers ORESTES is shaken and distraught.)

ORESTES.
How, brother? And is this the sanctuary
At last, for which we sailed from Argolis?

PYLADES.
For sure, Orestes. Seest thou not it is?

ORESTES.
The altar, too, where Hellene blood is shed.

PYLADES.
How like long hair those blood-stains, tawny red!

ORESTES.
And spoils of slaughtered men—there by the thatch.

PYLADES.
Aye, first-fruits of the harvest, when they catch
Their strangers!—'Tis a place to search with care

[He searches, while ORESTES sits.]

ORESTES.

O God, where hast thou brought me? What new snare
Is this?—I slew my mother; I avenged
My father at thy bidding; I have ranged
A homeless world, hunted by shapes of pain,
And circling trod in mine own steps again.
At last I stood once more before thy throne
And cried thee question, what thing should be done
To end these miseries, wherein I reel
Through Hellas, mad, lashed like a burning wheel;
And thou didst bid me seek ... what land but this
Of Tauri, where thy sister Artemis
Her altar hath, and seize on that divine
Image which fell, men say, into this shrine
From heaven. This I must seize by chance or plot
Or peril—clearer word was uttered not—
And bear to Attic earth. If this be done,
I should have peace from all my malison.

   Lo, I have done thy will. I have pierced the seas
Where no Greek man may live.—Ho, Pylades,
Sole sharer of my quest: hast seen it all?
What can we next? Thou seest this circuit wall
Enormous? Must we climb the public stair,
With all men watching? Shall we seek somewhere
Some lock to pick, some secret bolt or bar—
Of all which we know nothing? Where we are,
If one man mark us, if they see us prize
The gate, or think of entrance anywise,
'Tis death.—We still have time to fly for home:
Back to the galley quick, ere worse things come!

PYLADES.

To fly we dare not, brother. 'Twere a thing
Not of our custom; and ill work, to bring
God's word to such reviling.—Let us leave
The temple now, and gather in some cave
Where glooms the cool sea ripple. But not where
The ship lies; men might chance to see her there
And tell some chief; then certain were our doom.

But when the fringed eye of Night be come
Then we must dare, by all ways foul or fine,
To thieve that wondrous Image from its shrine.
Ah, see; far up, between each pair of beams
A hollow one might creep through! Danger gleams
Like sunshine to a brave man's eyes, and fear
Of what may be is no help anywhere.

ORESTES.
Aye; we have never braved these leagues of way
To falter at the end. See, I obey
Thy words. They are ever wise. Let us go mark
Some cavern, to lie hid till fall of dark.
God will not suffer that bad things be stirred
To mar us now, and bring to naught the word
Himself hath spoke. Aye, and no peril brings
Pardon for turning back to sons of kings.

[They go out towards the shore. After they are gone, enter gradually the
WOMEN]

CHORUS.
Peace! Peace upon all who dwell
By the Sister Rocks that clash in the swell
   Of the Friendless Seas.

  O Child of Leto, thou,
  Dictynna mountain-born,
  To the cornice gold-inlaid
  To the pillared sanctities,
  We come in the cold of morn,
  We come with virgin brow,
  Pure as our oath was sworn,
  Handmaids of thine handmaid
  Who holdeth the stainless keys,

  From Hellas, that once was ours,
  We come before thy gate,
  From the land of the western seas,
  The horses and the towers,

The wells and the garden trees,
And the seats where our fathers sate.

LEADER.
What tidings, ho? With what intent
  Hast called me to thy shrine and thee,
  O child of him who crossed the sea
To Troy with that great armament,
The thousand prows, the myriad swords?
I come, O child of Atreid Lords.

[IPHIGENIA, followed by ATTENDANTS, comes from the
Temple.]

IPHIGENIA.
  Alas, O maidens mine,
  I am filled full of tears:
  My heart filled with the beat
  Of tears, as of dancing feet,
A lyreless joyless line,
And music meet for the dead.

For a whisper is in mine ears,
By visions borne on the breath
Of the Night that now is fled,
Of a brother gone to death.
Oh sorrow and weeping sore,
  For the house that no more is,
For the dead that were kings of yore
  And the labour of Argolis!

[She begins the Funeral Rite.]

O Spirit, thou unknown,
  Who bearest on dark wings
My brother, my one, mine own,
  I bear drink-offerings,
And the cup that bringeth ease
  Flowing through Earth's deep breast;
Milk of the mountain kine,
The hallowed gleam of wine,

The toil of murmuring bees:
  By these shall the dead have rest.

To an ATTENDANT.

The golden goblet let me pour,
And that which Hades thirsteth for.

O branch of Agamemnon's tree
  Beneath the earth, as to one dead,
This cup of love I pour to thee.
  Oh, pardon, that I may not shed

One lock of hair to wreathe thy tomb,
  One tear: so far, so far am I
From what to me and thee was home,
  And where in all men's fantasy,
  Butchered, O God! I also lie.

CHORUS.

Woe; woe: I too with refluent melody,
  An echo wild of the dirges of the Asian,
I, thy bond maiden, cry to answer thee:
  The music that lieth hid in lamentation,
The song that is heard in the deep hearts of the dead,
  That the Lord of dead men 'mid his dancing singeth,
  And never joy-cry, never joy it bringeth;
  Woe for the house of Kings in desolation,
Woe for the light of the sceptre vanished.

From kings in Argos of old, from joyous kings,
      The beginning came:
Then peril swift upon peril, flame on flame:
The dark and wheeling coursers, as wild with wings,
The cry of one betrayed on a drowning shore,
The sun that blanched in heaven, the world that
      changed—
Evil on evil and none alone!—deranged
By the Golden Lamb and the wrong grown ever more;
Blood following blood, sorrow on sorrow sore!

So come the dead of old, the dead in wrath,
Back on the seed of the high Tantalidae;
Surely the Spirit of Life an evil path
        Hath hewed for thee.
IPHIGENIA.
From the beginning the Spirit of my life
Was an evil spirit. Alas for my mother's zone,
And the night that bare me! From the beginning
  Strife,
As a book to read, Fate gave me for mine own.
They wooed a bride for the strikers down of Troy—
Thy first-born, Mother: was it for this, thy prayer?—
A hind of slaughter to die in a father's snare,
Gift of a sacrifice where none hath joy.

  They set me on a royal wane;
    Down the long sand they led me on,
  A bride new-decked, a bride of bane,
    In Aulis to the Nereid's son.
  And now estranged for evermore
    Beyond the far estranging foam
  I watch a flat and herbless shore,
    Unloved, unchilded, without home
  Or city: never more to meet
    For Hera's dance with Argive maids,
  Nor round the loom 'mid singing sweet
    Make broideries and storied braids,
  Of writhing giants overthrown
  And clear-eyed Pallas ... All is gone!
  Red hands and ever-ringing ears:
  The blood of men that friendless die,
  The horror of the strangers' cry
  Unheard, the horror of their tears.

  But now, let even that have rest:
  I weep for him in Argos slain,
    The brother whom I knew, Ah me,
    A babe, a flower; and yet to be—
    There on his mother's arms and breast—
    The crowned Orestes, lord of men!

LEADER OF THE CHORUS.
Stay, yonder from some headland of the sea
There comes—methinks a herdsman, seeking thee.

(Enter a HERDSMAN. IPHIGENIA is still on her knees.)

HERDSMAN.
Daughter of Clytemnestra and her king,
Give ear! I bear news of a wondrous thing.

IPHIGENIA.
What news, that should so mar my obsequies?

HERDSMAN.
A ship hath passed the blue Symplegades,
And here upon our coast two men are thrown,
Young, bold, good slaughter for the altar-stone
Of Artemis!

[SHE RISES.]

    Make all the speed ye may;
'Tis not too much. The blood-bowl and the spray!

IPHIGENIA.
Men of what nation? Doth their habit show?

HERDSMAN.
Hellenes for sure, but that is all we know.

IPHIGENIA.
No name? No other clue thine ear could seize?

HERDSMAN.
We heard one call his comrade "Pylades."

IPHIGENIA.
Yes. And the man who spoke—his name was what?

HERDSMAN.
None of us heard. I think they spoke it not.

IPHIGENIA.
How did ye see them first, how make them fast?

HERDSMAN.
Down by the sea, just where the surge is cast ...

IPHIGENIA.
The sea? What is the sea to thee and thine?

HERDSMAN.
We came to wash our cattle in the brine.

IPHIGENIA.
Go back, and tell how they were taken; show
The fashion of it, for I fain would know
All.—'Tis so long a time, and never yet,
Never, hath Greek blood made this altar wet.

HERDSMAN.
We had brought our forest cattle where the seas
Break in long tides from the Symplegades.
A bay is there, deep caten by the surge
And hollowed clear, with cover by the verge
Where purple-fishers camp. These twain were there
When one of mine own men, a forager,
Spied them, and tiptoed whispering back: "God save
Us now! Two things unearthly by the wave
Sitting!" We looked, and one of pious mood
Raised up his hands to heaven and praying stood:
"Son of the white Sea Spirit, high in rule,
Storm-lord Palaemon, Oh, be merciful:
Or sit ye there the warrior twins of Zeus,
Or something loved of Him, from whose great thews
Was-born the Nereids' fifty-fluted choir."
  Another, flushed with folly and the fire
Of lawless daring, laughed aloud and swore
'Twas shipwrecked sailors skulking on the shore,
Our rule and custom here being known, to slay
All strangers. And most thought this was the way

To follow, and seek out for Artemis
The blood-gift of our people.

              Just at this
One of the strangers started from his seat,
And stood, and upward, downward, with a beat
His head went, and he groaned, and all his arm
Trembled. Then, as a hunter gives alarm,
He shrieked, stark mad and raving: "Pylades,
Dost see her there?—And there—Oh, no one sees!—
A she-dragon of Hell, and all her head
Agape with fanged asps, to bite me dead.
She hath no face, but somewhere from her cloak
Bloweth a wind of fire and bloody smoke:
The wings' beat fans it: in her arms, Ah see!
My mother, dead grey stone, to cast on me
And crush … Help, help! They crowd on me
  behind …"

  No shapes at all were there. 'Twas his sick mind
Which turned the herds that lowed and barking hounds
That followed, to some visionary sounds
Of Furies. For ourselves, we did but sit
And watch in silence, wondering if the fit
Would leave him dead. When suddenly out shone
His sword, and like a lion he leaped upon
Our herds, to fight his Furies! Flank and side
He stabbed and smote them, till the foam was dyed
Red at the waves' edge. Marry, when we saw
The cattle hurt and falling, no more law
We gave, but sprang to arms and blew the horn
For help—so strong they looked and nobly born
For thralls like us to meet, that pair unknown.

  Well, a throng gathered ere much time was gone;
When suddenly the whirl of madness slips
From off him and he falls, quite weak, his lips
Dropping with foam. When once we saw him fall
So timely, we were at him one and all
To pelt and smite. The other watched us come,

But knelt and wiped those lips all dank with foam
And tended the sick body, while he held
His cloak's good web above him for a shield;
So cool he was to ward off every stone
And all the while care for that stricken one.

  Then rose the fallen man, calm now and grave,
Looked, and saw battle bursting like a wave
That bursts, and knew that peril close at hand
Which now is come, and groaned. On every hand
We stood, and stoned and stoned, and ceased not. Aye,
'Twas then we heard that fearful battle-cry:
"Ho, Pylades, 'tis death! But let it be
A gallant death! Draw sword and follow me."

  When those two swords came flashing, up the glen
Through the loose rocks we scattered back; but when
One band was flying, down by rocks and trees
Came others pelting: did they turn on these,
Back stole the first upon them, stone on stone.
'Twas past belief: of all those shots not one
Struck home. The goddess kept her fated prey
Perfect. Howbeit, at last we made our way
Right, left and round behind them on the sands,
And rushed, and beat the swords out of their hands,
So tired they scarce could stand. Then to the king
We bore them both, and he, not tarrying,
Sends them to thee, to touch with holy spray—
And then the blood-bowl!

                    I have heard thee pray,
Priestess, ere now for such a draft as this.
Aye, slay but these two chiefs to Artemis
And Hellas shall have paid thy debt, and know
What blood was spilt in Aulis long ago.

LEADER.
I marvel that one mad, whoe'er he be,
Should sail from Hellas to the Friendless Sea.

IPHIGENIA.
'Tis well. Let thy hand bring them, and mine own
Shall falter not till here God's will be done.

[EXIT HERDSMAN.]

O suffering heart, not fierce thou wast of old
To shipwrecked men. Nay, pities manifold
Held thee in fancy homeward, lest thy hand
At last should fall on one of thine own land.
But now, for visions that have turned to stone
My heart, to know Orestes sees the sun
No more, a cruel woman waits you here,
Whoe'er ye be, and one without a tear.
  'Tis true: I know by mine own evil will:
One long in pain, if things more suffering still
Fall to his hand, will hate them for his own
Torment ... And no great wind hath ever blown,
No ship from God hath passed the Clashing Gate,
To bring me Helen, who hath earned my hate,
And Menelaus, till I mocked their prayers
In this new Aulis, that is mine, not theirs:
Where Greek hands held me lifted, like a beast
For slaughter, and my throat bled. And the priest
My father! ... Not one pang have I forgot.
  Ah me, the blind half-prisoned arms I shot
This way and that, to find his beard, his knees,
Groping and wondering: "Father, what are these
For bridal rites? My mother even now
Mid Argive women sings for me, whom thou ...
What dost thou? She sings happy songs, and all
Is dance and sound of piping in the hall;
And here ... Is he a vampyre, is he one
That fattens on the dead, thy Peleus' son—
Whose passion shaken like a torch before
My leaping chariot, lured me to this shore
To wed—"
        Ah me! And I had hid my face,
Burning, behind my veil. I would not press
Orestes to my arms ... who now is slain! ...

I would not kiss my sister's lips again,
For shame and fulness of the heart to meet
My bridegroom. All my kisses, all my sweet
Words were stored up and hid: I should come back
So soon to Argos!
        And thou, too: alack,
Brother, if dead thou art, from what high things
Thy youth is outcast, and the pride of kings
Fallen!
    And this the goddess deemeth good!
If ever mortal hand be dark with blood;
Nay, touch a new-made mother or one slain
In war, her ban is on him. 'Tis a stain
She driveth from her outer walls; and then
Herself doth drink this blood of slaughtered men?
Could ever Leto, she of the great King
Beloved, be mother to so gross a thing?
These tales be lies, false as those feastings wild
Of Tantalus and Gods that tore a child.
This land of murderers to its god hath given
Its own lust; evil dwelleth not in heaven.

[SHE GOES INTO THE TEMPLE.]

CHORUS.

Dark of the sea, dark of the sea, [STROPHE 1.]
  Gates of the warring water,
One, in the old time, conquered you,
A winged passion that burst the blue,
When the West was shut and the Dawn lay free
  To the pain of Inachus' daughter.
But who be these, from where the rushes blow
On pale Eurotas, from pure Dirce's flow,
  That turn not neither falter,
Seeking Her land, where no man breaketh bread,
Her without pity, round whose virgin head
Blood on the pillars rusts from long ago,
  Blood on the ancient altar.
                [ANTISTROPHE 1.]

A flash of the foam, a flash of the foam,
  A wave on the oarblade welling,
And out they passed to the heart of the blue:
A chariot shell that the wild winds drew.
Is it for passion of gold they come,
  Or pride to make great their dwelling?

For sweet is Hope, yea, to much mortal woe
So sweet that none may turn from it nor go,
  Whom once the far voice calleth,
To wander through fierce peoples and the gleam
Of desolate seas, in every heart a dream:
And these she maketh empty die, and, lo,
  To that man's hand she falleth.

[STROPHE 2.]

Through the Clashing Rocks they burst:
  They passed by the Cape unsleeping
Of Phineus' sons accurst:
They ran by the star-lit bay
  Upon magic surges sweeping,
Where folk on the waves astray
Have seen, through the gleaming grey,
Ring behind ring, men say,
  The dance of the old Sea's daughters.

The guiding oar abaft
  It rippled and it dinned,
And now the west wind laughed
  And now the south-west wind;
And the sail was full in flight,
And they passed by the Island White:

Birds, birds, everywhere,
White as the foam, light as the air;
And ghostly Achilles raceth there,
  Far in the Friendless Waters.
                    [ANTISTROPHE 1.]
Ah, would that Leda's child ...

(So prayeth the priestess maiden)
From Troy, that she beguiled,
Hither were borne, to know
  What sin on her soul is laden!
Hair twisted, throat held low,
Head back for the blood to flow,
To die by the sword. ... Ah no!
  One hope my soul yet hideth.

A sail, a sail from Greece,
  Fearless to cross the sea,
With ransom and with peace
  To my sick captivity.
O home, to see thee still,
And the old walls on the hill!

Dreams, dreams, gather to me!
Bear me on wings over the sea;
O joy of the night, to slave and free,
  One good thing that abideth!

LEADER.
  But lo, the twain whom Thoas sends,
    Their arms in bondage grasped sore;
    Strange offering this, to lay before
  The Goddess! Hold your peace, O friends.

Onward, still onward, to this shrine
  They lead the first-fruits of the Greek.
  'Twas true, the tale he came to speak,
That watcher of the mountain kine.

O holy one, if it afford
  Thee joy, what these men bring to thee,
  Take thou their sacrifice, which we,
By law of Hellas, hold abhorred.

[Enter ORESTES and PYLADES, bound, and guarded by
taurians. re-enter IPHIGENIA.]

IPHIGENIA.
So be it.
My foremost care must be that nothing harms
The temple's holy rule.—Untie their arms.
That which is hallowed may no more be bound.
You, to the shrine within! Let all be found
As the law bids, and as we need this day.

[ORESTES and PYLADES are set free; some
ATTENDANTS go into the temple.]

Ah me!
What mother then was yours, O strangers, say,
And father? And your sister, if you have
A sister: both at once, so young and brave
To leave her brotherless! Who knows when heaven
May send that fortune? For to none is given
To know the coming nor the end of woe;
So dark is God, and to great darkness go
His paths, by blind chance mazed from our ken.
  Whence are ye come, O most unhappy men?
From some far home, methinks, ye have found this shore
And far shall stay from home for evermore.

ORESTES.
Why weepest thou, woman, to make worse the smart
Of that which needs must be, whoe'er thou art?
I count it not for gentleness, when one
Who means to slay, seeks first to make undone
By pity that sharp dread. Nor praise I him,
With hope long dead, who sheddeth tears to dim
The pain that grips him close. The evil so
Is doubled into twain. He doth but show
His feeble heart, and, as he must have died,
Dies.—Let ill fortune float upon her tide
And weep no more for us. What way this land
Worships its god we know and understand.

IPHIGENIA.
Say first ... which is it men call Pylades?

ORESTES.
'Tis this man's name, if that will give thee ease.

IPHIGENIA.
From what walled town of Hellas cometh he?

ORESTES.
Enough!—How would the knowledge profit thee?

IPHIGENIA.
Are ye two brethren of one mother born?

ORESTES.
No, not in blood. In love we are brothers sworn.

IPHIGENIA.
Thou also hast a name: tell me thereof.

ORESTES.
Call me Unfortunate. 'Tis name enough.

IPHIGENIA.
I asked not that. Let that with Fortune lie.

ORESTES.
Fools cannot laugh at them that nameless die.

IPHIGENIA.
Why grudge me this? Hast thou such mighty fame?

ORESTES.
My body, if thou wilt, but not my name.

IPHIGENIA.
Nor yet the land of Greece where thou wast bred?

ORESTES.
What gain to have told it thee, when I am dead?

IPHIGENIA.
Nay: why shouldst thou deny so small a grace?

ORESTES.
Know then, great Argos was my native place.

IPHIGENIA.
Stranger! The truth! … From Argos art thou come?

ORESTES.
Mycenae, once a rich land, was my home.

IPHIGENIA.
'Tis banishment that brings thee here—or what?

ORESTES.
A kind of banishment, half forced, half sought.

IPHIGENIA.
Wouldst thou but tell me all I need of thee!

ORESTES.
'Twere not much added to my misery.

IPHIGENIA.
From Argos! … Oh, how sweet to see thee here!

ORESTES.
Enjoy it, then. To me 'tis sorry cheer.

IPHIGENIA.
Thou knowest the name of Troy? Far doth it flit.

ORESTES.
Would God I had not; nay, nor dreamed of it.

IPHIGENIA.
Men fable it is fallen beneath the sword?

ORESTES.
Fallen it is. Thou hast heard no idle word.

IPHIGENIA.
Fallen! At last!—And Helen taken too?

ORESTES.
Aye; on an evil day for one I knew.

IPHIGENIA.
Where is she? I too have some anger stored ...

ORESTES.
In Sparta! Once more happy with her lord!

IPHIGENIA.
Oh. hated of all Greece, not only me!

ORESTES.
I too have tasted of her wizardry.

IPHIGENIA.
And came the armies home, as the tales run?

ORESTES.
To answer that were many tales in one.

IPHIGENIA.
Oh, give me this hour full! Thou wilt soon die.

ORESTES.
Ask, if such longing holds thee. I will try.

IPHIGENIA.
A seer called Calchas! Did he ever come ...?

ORESTES.

Calchas is dead, as the news went at home.

IPHIGENIA.

Good news, ye gods!—Odysseus, what of him?

ORESTES.

Not home yet, but still living, as men deem.

IPHIGENIA.

Curse him! And may he see his home no more.

ORESTES.

Why curse him? All his house is stricken sore.

IPHIGENIA.

How hath the Nereid's son, Achilles, sped?

ORESTES.

Small help his bridal brought him! He is dead.

IPHIGENIA.

A fierce bridal, so the sufferers tell!

ORESTES.

Who art thou, questioning of Greece so well?

IPHIGENIA.

I was Greek. Evil caught me long ago.

ORESTES.
Small wonder, then, thou hast such wish to know.

IPHIGENIA.
That war-lord, whom they call so high in bliss...

ORESTES.
None such is known to me. What name was his?

IPHIGENIA.
They called him Agamemnon, Atreus' son.

ORESTES.
I know not. Cease.—My questioning is done.

IPHIGENIA.
'Twill be such joy to me! How fares he? Tell!

ORESTES.
Dead. And hath wrecked another's life as well.

IPHIGENIA.
Dead? By what dreadful fortune? Woe is me!

ORESTES.
Why sighst thou? Had he any link with thee?

IPHIGENIA.
I did but think of his old joy and pride.

ORESTES.
His own wife foully stabbed him, and he died.

IPHIGENIA.
O God!
I pity her that slew ... and him that slew.

ORESTES.
Now cease thy questions. Add no word thereto.

IPHIGENIA.
But one word. Lives she still, that hapless wife?

ORESTES.
No. Her own son, her first-born, took her life.

IPHIGENIA.
O shipwrecked house! What thought was in his brain?

ORESTES.
Justice on her, to avenge his father slain.

IPHIGENIA.
Alas!
A bad false duty bravely hath he wrought.

ORESTES.
Yet God, for all his duty, helps him not.

IPHIGENIA.
And not one branch of Atreus' tree lives on?

ORESTES.
Electra lives, unmated and alone.

IPHIGENIA.
The child they slaughtered ... is there word of her?

ORESTES.
Why, no, save that she died in Aulis there.

IPHIGENIA.
Poor child! Poor father, too, who killed and lied!

ORESTES.
For a bad woman's worthless sake she died.

IPHIGENIA.
The dead king's son, lives he in Argos still?

ORESTES.
He lives, now here, now nowhere, bent with ill.

IPHIGENIA.
O dreams, light dreams, farewell! Ye too were lies.

ORESTES.
Aye; the gods too, whom mortals deem so wise,
Are nothing clearer than some winged dream;
And all their ways, like man's ways, but a stream
Of turmoil. He who cares to suffer least,
Not blind, as fools are blinded, by a priest,
Goes straight... to what death, those who know him know.

LEADER.
We too have kinsmen dear, but, being low,
None heedeth, live they still or live they not.

IPHIGENIA (WITH SUDDEN IMPULSE).
Listen! For I am fallen upon a thought,
Strangers, of some good use to you and me,
Both. And 'tis thus most good things come to be,
When different eyes hold the same for fair.

Stranger, if I can save thee, wilt thou bear
To Argos and the friends who loved my youth
Some word? There is a tablet which, in truth
For me and mine ill works, a prisoner wrote,
Ta'en by the king in war. He knew 'twas not
My will that craved for blood, but One on high
Who holds it righteous her due prey shall die.
And since that day no Greek hath ever come
Whom I could save and send to Argos home
With prayer for help to any friend: but thou,
I think, dost loathe me not; and thou dost know
Mycenae and the names that fill my heart.
Help me! Be saved! Thou also hast thy part,
Sending Completed Page, Please Wait ...

IPHIGENIA.
'Tis I. This altar's spell is over me.

ORESTES.
A grievous office and unblest, O maid.

IPHIGENIA.
What dare I do? The law must be obeyed.

ORESTES.
A girl to hold a sword and stab men dead!

IPHIGENIA.
I shall but sign the water on thy head.

ORESTES.
And who shall strike me, if I needs must ask?

IPHIGENIA.
There be within these vaults who know their task.

ORESTES.
My grave, when they have finished their desire?

IPHIGENIA.
A great gulf of the rock, and holy fire.

ORESTES.
Woe's me!
Would that my sister's hand could close mine eyes!

IPHIGENIA.
Alas, she dwelleth under distant skies,
Unhappy one, and vain is all thy prayer.
Yet, Oh, them art from Argos: all of care
That can be, I will give and fail thee not.
Rich raiment to thy burial shall be brought,
And oil to cool thy pyre in golden floods,
And sweet that from a thousand mountain buds
The murmuring bee hath garnered, I will throw
To die with thee in fragrance. ...
                    I must go
And seek the tablet from the Goddess' room
Within.—Oh, do not hate me for my doom!

Watch them, ye servitors, but leave them free.

It may be, past all hoping, it may be,
My word shall sail to Argos, to his hand
Whom most I love. How joyous will he stand
To know, past hope, that here on the world's rim
His dead are living, and cry out for him!

[She goes into the Temple.]

CHORUS.
Alas, we pity thee; surely we pity thee: [Strophe.]
  Who art given over to the holy water,
    The drops that fall deadly as drops of blood.

ORESTES.
I weep not, ye Greek maidens: but farewell.

CHORUS.

[ANTISTROPHE.]

29

Aye, and rejoice with thee; surely rejoice with thee,
  Thou happy rover from the place of slaughter;
    Thy foot shall stand again where thy father's
      stood.

PYLADES.
While he I love must die? 'Tis miserable.

DIVERS WOMEN OF THE CHORUS.
A. Alas, the deathward faring of the lost!
B. Woe, woe; thou too shalt move to misery.
C Which one shall suffer most?
D. My heart is torn by two words evenly,
    For thee should I most sorrow, or for thee?

ORESTES.
By heaven, is THY thought, Pylades, like mine?

PYLADES.
O friend, I cannot speak.—But what is thine?

ORESTES.
Who can the damsel be? How Greek her tone
Of question, all of Ilion overthrown,
And how the kings came back, the wizard flame
Of Calchas, and Achilles' mighty name,
And ill-starred Agamemnon. With a keen
Pity she spoke, and asked me of his queen
And children … The strange woman comes from
    there
By race, an Argive maid.—What aileth her
With tablets, else, and questionings as though
Her own heart beat with Argos' joy or woe?

PYLADES.
Thy speech is quicker, friend, else I had said
The same; though surely all men visited
By ships have heard the fall of the great kings.
But let that be: I think of other things …

ORESTES.
What? If thou hast need of me, let it be said.

PYLADES.
I cannot live for shame if thou art dead.
I sailed together with thee; let us die
Together. What a coward slave were I,
Creeping through Argos and from glen to glen
Of wind-torn Phocian hills! And most of men—
For most are bad—will whisper how one day
I left my friend to die and made my way
Home. They will say I watched the sinking breath
Of thy great house and plotted for thy death
To wed thy sister, climb into thy throne…
I dread, I loathe it.—Nay, all ways but one
Are shut. My last breath shall go forth with thine,
Thy bloody sword, thy gulf of fire be mine
Also. I love thee and I dread men's scorn.

ORESTES.
Peace from such thoughts! My burden can be borne;
But where one pain sufficeth, double pain
I will not bear. Nay, all that scorn and stain
That fright thee, on mine own head worse would be
If I brought death on him who toiled for me.
It is no bitter thing for such an one
As God will have me be, at last to have done
With living. THOU art happy; thy house lies
At peace with God, unstained in men's eyes;
Mine is all evil fate and evil life …
Nay, thou once safe, my sister for thy wife—
So we agreed:—in sons of hers and thine
My name will live, nor Agamemnon's line
Be blurred for ever like an evil scroll.
Back! Rule thy land! Let life be in thy soul!
And when thou art come to Hellas, and the plain
Of Argos where the horsemen ride, again—
Give me thy hand!—I charge thee, let there be
Some death-mound and a graven stone for me.
My sister will go weep thereat, and shear

A tress or two. Say how I ended here,
Slain by a maid of Argolis, beside
God's altar, in mine own blood purified.

   And fare thee well. I have no friend like thee
For truth and love, O boy that played with me,
And hunted on Greek hills, O thou on whom
Hath lain the hardest burden of my doom!
Farewell. The Prophet and the Lord of Lies
Hath done his worst. Far out from Grecian skies
With craft forethought he driveth me, to die
Where none may mark how ends his prophecy!
I trusted in his word. I gave him all
My heart. I slew my mother at his call;
For which things now he casts me here to die.

PYLADES.
Thy tomb shall fail thee not. Thy sister I
Will guard for ever. I, O stricken sore,
Who loved thee living and shall love thee more
Dead. But for all thou standest on the brink,
God's promise hath not yet destroyed thee. Think!
How oft, how oft the darkest hour of ill
Breaks brightest into dawn, if Fate but will!

ORESTES.
Enough. Nor god nor man can any more
Aid me. The woman standeth at the door.

[enter IPHIGENIA from the Temple.]

IPHIGENIA.
Go ye within; and have all things of need
In order set for them that do the deed.
There wait my word.

[ATTENDANTS go in.]

      Ye strangers, here I hold
The many-lettered tablet, fold on fold.
Yet … one thing still. No man, once unafraid

And safe, remembereth all the vows he made
In fear of death. My heart misgiveth me,
Lest he who bears my tablet, once gone free,
Forget me here and set my charge at naught.

ORESTES.
What wouldst thou, then? Thou hast some troubling thought.

IPHIGENIA.
His sworn oath let him give, to bear this same
Tablet to Argos, to the friend I name.

ORESTES.
And if he give this oath, wilt thou swear too?

IPHIGENIA.
What should I swear to do or not to do?

ORESTES.
Send him from Tauris safe and free from ill.

IPHIGENIA.
I promise. How else could he do my will?

ORESTES.
The King will suffer this?

IPHIGENIA.
                    Yes: I can bend
The King, and set upon his ship thy friend.

ORESTES.
Choose then what oath is best, and he will swear.

IPHIGENIA (to PYLADES, who has come up to her).
Say: "To thy friend this tablet I will bear."

PYLADES (TAKING THE TABLET).
Good. I will bear this tablet to thy friend.

IPHIGENIA.
And I save thee beyond this kingdom's end.

PYLADES.
What god dost thou invoke to witness this?

IPHIGENIA.
Her in whose house I labour, Artemis.

PYLADES.
And I the Lord of Heaven, eternal Zeus.

IPHIGENIA.
And if thou fail me, or thine oath abuse ...?

PYLADES.
May I see home no more. And thou, what then?

IPHIGENIA.
May this foot never tread Greek earth again.

PYLADES.
But stay: there is one chance we have forgot.

IPHIGENIA.
A new oath can be sworn, if this serve not.

PYLADES.
In one case set me free. Say I be crossed
With shipwreck, and, with ship and tablet lost
And all I bear, my life be saved alone:
Let not this oath be held a thing undone,
To curse me.

IPHIGENIA.
          Nay, then, many ways are best
To many ends. The words thou carriest
Enrolled and hid beneath that tablet's rim,
I will repeat to thee, and thou to him
I look for. Safer so. If the scrip sail
Unhurt to Greece, itself will tell my tale
Unaided: if it drown in some wide sea,
Save but thyself, my words are saved with thee.

PYLADES.
For thy sake and for mine 'tis fairer so.
Now let me hear his name to whom I go
In Argolis, and how my words should run.

IPHIGENIA (REPEATING THE WORDS BY HEART).
Say: "To Orestes, Agamemnon's son
She that was slain in Aulis, dead to Greece
Yet quick, Iphigenia sendeth peace:"

ORESTES.
Iphigenia! Where? Back from the dead?

IPHIGENIA.
'Tis I. But speak not, lest thou break my thread.—
"Take me to Argos, brother, ere I die,
Back from the Friendless Peoples and the high
Altar of Her whose bloody rites I wreak."

ORESTES (ASIDE).
Where am I, Pylades? How shall I speak?

IPHIGENIA.
"Else one in grief forsaken shall, like shame,
Haunt thee."

PYLADES (aside).
    Orestes!

IPHIGENIA (overhearing him).
    Yes: that is the name.

PYLADES.
Ye Gods above!

IPHIGENIA.
    Why callest thou on God
For words of mine?

PYLADES.
    'Tis nothing. 'Twas a road

My thoughts had turned. Speak on.—No need for us
To question; we shall hear things marvellous.

IPHIGENIA.
Tell him that Artemis my soul did save,
I wot not how, and to the altar gave
A fawn instead; the which my father slew,
Not seeing, deeming that the sword he drew
Struck me. But she had borne me far away
And left me in this land.—I charge thee, say
So much. It all is written on the scroll.

PYLADES.
An easy charge thou layest on my soul,
A glad oath on thine own. I wait no more,
But here fulfil the service that I swore.
  Orestes, take this tablet which I bear
To thine own hand, thy sister's messenger.

ORESTES.
I take it, but I reck not of its scrip
Nor message. Too much joy is at my lip.
Sister! Beloved! Wildered though I be,
My arms believe not, yet they crave for thee.
Now, filled with wonder, give me my delight!

[he goes to embrace her. she stands speechless.]

LEADER.
Stranger, forbear! No living man hath right
To touch that robe. The Goddess were defiled!

ORESTES.
O Sister mine, O my dead father's child,
Agamemnon's child; take me and have no fear,
Beyond all dreams 'tis I thy brother here.

IPHIGENIA.
My brother? Thou? ... Peace! Mock at me no more.
Argos is bright with him and Nauplia's shore.

ORESTES.
Unhappy one! Thou hast no brother there.

IPHIGENIA.
Orestes ... thou? Whom Clytemnestra bare?

ORESTES.
To Atreus' firstborn son, thy sire and mine.

IPHIGENIA.
Thou sayst it: Oh, give me some proof, some sign!

ORESTES.
What sign thou wilt. Ask anything from home.

IPHIGENIA.
Nay, thou speak: 'tis from thee the sign should come.

ORESTES.
That will I.—First, old tales Electra told.
Thou knowest how Pelops' princes warred of old?

IPHIGENIA.
I know: the Golden Lamb that wrought their doom.

ORESTES.
Thine own hand wove that story on the loom...

IPHIGENIA.
How sweet! Thou movest near old memories.

ORESTES.
With a great Sun back beaten in the skies.

IPHIGENIA.
Fine linen threads I used. The memories come.

ORESTES.
And mother gave thee shrift-water from home
For Aulis ...

IPHIGENIA.
    I remember. Not so fair
A day did drink that water!

ORESTES.
                And thine hair
They brought us for thy dying gift, and gave
To mother.

IPHIGENIA.
    Yes: for record on the grave
I sent it, where this head should never lie.

ORESTES.
Another token, seen of mine own eye.
The ancient lance that leapt in Pelops' hand,
To win his bride, the virgin of the land,
And smite Oenomaus, in thy chamber hid ...

IPHIGENIA (falling into his arms).
Beloved! Oh, no other, for indeed
Beloved art thou! In mine arms at last,
    Orestes far away.

ORESTES.
And thou in mine, the evil dreaming past,
    Back from the dead this day!
Yet through the joy tears, tears and sorrow loud
Are o'er mine eyes and thine eyes, like a cloud.

IPHIGENIA.
    Is this the babe I knew,
The little babe, light lifted like a bird?
O heart of mine, too blest for any word,
    What shall I say or do?
Beyond all wonders, beyond stories heard,
    This joy is here and true.

ORESTES.
Could we but stay thus joined for evermore!

IPHIGENIA.
A joy is mine I may not understand,
Friends, and a fear, lest sudden from my hand
　　This dream will melt and soar
Up to the fiery skies from whence it came.
O Argos land, O hearth and holy flame
　　That old Cyclopes lit,
I bless ye that he lives, that he is grown,
A light and strength, my brother and mine own;
　　I bless your name for it.

ORESTES.
One blood we are; so much is well. But Fate,
Sister, hath not yet made us fortunate.

IPHIGENIA.
O most unfortunate! Did I not feel,
Whose father, misery-hearted, at my bare
　　Throat held the steel?

ORESTES.
Woe's me! Methinks even now I see thee there.

IPHIGENIA.
No love-song of Achilles! Crafty arms
　　Drew me to that cold sleep,
And tears, blind tears amid the altar psalms
　　And noise of them that weep—
That was my cleansing!

ORESTES.
　　　　　My heart too doth bleed,
To think our father wrought so dire a deed.

IPHIGENIA.
My life hath known no father. Any road
　　To any end may run,
As god's will drives; else ...

ORESTES.
                    Else, unhappy one,
Thyself had spilt this day thy brother's blood!

IPHIGENIA.
Ah God, my cruel deed! ... 'Twas horrible.
'Twas horrible ... O brother! Did my heart
    Endure it? ... And things fell
Right by so frail a chance; and here thou art.
    Bloody my hand had been,
    My heart heavy with sin.
    And now, what end cometh?
    Shall Chance yet comfort me,
    Finding a way for thee
    Back from the Friendless Strand,
      Back from the place of death—
    Ere yet the slayers come
    And thy blood sink in the sand—
    Home unto Argos, home? ...
  Hard heart, so swift to slay,
  Is there to life no way? ...

    No ship! ... And how by land? ...
      A rush of feet
    Out to the waste alone.
      Nay: 'twere to meet
    Death, amid tribes unknown
    And trackless ways of the waste ...
    Surely the sea were best.
    Back by the narrow bar
      To the Dark Blue Gate! ...
    Ah God, too far, too far! ...
      Desolate! Desolate!

What god or man, what unimagined flame,
  Can cleave this road where no road is, and bring
To us last wrecks of Agamemnon's name,
    Peace from long suffering?

LEADER.
Lo, deeds of wonder and beyond surmise,
Not as tales told, but seen of mine own eyes.

PYLADES.
Men that have found the arms of those they love
Would fain long linger in the joy thereof.
But we, Orestes, have no respite yet
For tears or tenderness. Let us forget
All but the one word Freedom, calling us
To live, not die by altars barbarous.
Think not of joy in this great hour, nor lose
Fortune's first hold. Not thus do wise men use.

ORESTES.
I think that Fortune watcheth o'er our lives,
Surer than we. But well said: he who strives
Will find his gods strive for him equally.

IPHIGENIA.
He shall not check us so, nor baffle me
Of this one word. How doth Electra move
Through life? Ye twain are all I have to love.

ORESTES.
A wife and happy: this man hath her hand.

IPHIGENIA.
And what man's son is he, and of what land?

ORESTES.
Son of King Strophios he is called of men.

IPHIGENIA.
Whom Atreus' daughter wed?—My kinsman then.

ORESTES.
Our cousin, and my true and only friend.

IPHIGENIA.
He was not born, when I went to mine end.

ORESTES.
No, Strophios had no child for many a year.

IPHIGENIA.
I give thee hail, husband of one so dear.

ORESTES.
My more than kinsman, saviour in my need!

IPHIGENIA.
But mother ... Speak: how did ye dare that deed?

ORESTES.
Our father's wrongs ... But let that story be.

IPHIGENIA.
And she to slay her king! What cause had she?

ORESTES.
Forget her! ... And no tale for thee it is.

IPHIGENIA.
So be it.—And thou art Lord of Argolis?

ORESTES.
Our uncle rules. I walk an exile's ways.

IPHIGENIA.
Doth he so trample on our fallen days?

ORESTES.
Nay: there be those that drive me, Shapes of Dread.

IPHIGENIA.
Ah!
That frenzy on the shore! 'Tis as they said...

ORESTES.
They saw me in mine hour. It needs must be.

IPHIGENIA.
'Twas our dead mother's Furies hounding thee!

ORESTES.
My mouth is bloody with the curb they ride.

IPHIGENIA.
What brought thee here beyond the Friendless Tide?

ORESTES.
What leads me everywhere—Apollo's word.

IPHIGENIA.
Seeking what end?—Or may the tale be heard?

ORESTES.
Nay, I can tell thee all. It needs must be
The whole tale of my days of misery.
  When this sore evil that we speak not of
Lit on my hand, this way and that they drove
My body, till the God by diverse paths
Led me to Athens, that the nameless Wraths
Might bring me before judgment. For that land
A pure tribunal hath, where Ares' hand,
Red from an ancient stain, by Zeus was sent
For justice. Thither came I; and there went
God's hate before me, that at first no man
Would give me shelter. Then some few began
To pity, and set out for me aloof
One table. There I sate within their roof,
But without word they signed to me, as one
Apart, unspoken to, unlocked upon,
Lest touch of me should stain their meat and sup.
And every man in measure filled his cup
And gave me mine, and took their joy apart,
While I sat silent; for I had no heart
To upbraid the hosts that fed me. On I wrought
In my deep pain, feigning to mark them not.

  And now, men say, mine evil days are made
A rite among them and the cups are laid
Apart for each. The rule abideth still.

Howbeit, when I was come to Ares' Hill
They gave me judgment. On one stone I stood,
On one she that was eldest of the brood
That hunted me so long. And many a word
Touching my mother's death was spoke and heard,
Till Phoebus rose to save me. Even lay
The votes of Death and Life; when, lo, a sway
Of Pallas' arm, and free at last I stood
From that death grapple. But the Shapes of Blood—
Some did accept the judgment, and of grace
Consent to make their house beneath that place
In darkness. Others still consented not,
But clove to me the more, like bloodhounds hot
On the dying; till to Phoebus' house once more
I crept, and cast me starving on the floor
Facing the Holy Place, and made my cry:
"Lord Phoebus, here I am come, and here will die,
Unless thou save me, as thou hast betrayed."
And, lo, from out that dark and golden shade
A voice: "Go, seek the Taurian citadel:
Seize there the carven Artemis that fell
From heaven, and stablish it on Attic soil.
So comes thy freedom." [IPHIGENIA shrinks.]
                  Sister, in this toil

Help us!—If once that image I may win
That day shall end my madness and my sin:
And thou, to Argos o'er the sundering foam
My many-oared barque shall bear thee home.

  O sister loved and lost, O pitying face,
Help my great peril; help our father's race.
For lost am I and perished all the powers
Of Pelops, save that heavenly thing be ours!

LEADER.
Strange wrath of God hath fallen, like hot rain,
On Tantalus' house: he leadeth them through pain.

IPHIGENIA.

Long ere you came my heart hath yearned to be
In Argos, brother, and so near to thee:
But now—thy will is mine. To ease thy pain,
To lift our father's house to peace again,
And hate no more my murderers—aye,'tis good.
Perchance to clean this hand that sought thy blood,
And save my people...
               But the goddess' eyes,
How dream we to deceive them? Or what wise
Escape the King, when on his sight shall fall
The blank stone of the empty pedestal? ...
I needs must die ... What better can I do?

  And yet, one chance there is: could I but go
Together with the image: couldst thou bear
Both on the leaping seas! The risk were fair.
But how?

     Nay, I must wait then and be slain:
Thou shalt walk free in Argolis again,
And all life smile on thee ... Dearest, we need
Nor shrink from that. I shall by mine own deed
Have saved thee. And a man gone from the earth
Is wept for. Women are but little worth.

ORESTES.

My mother and then thou? It may not be.
This hand hath blood enough. I stand with thee
One-hearted here, be it for life or death,
And either bear thee, if God favoureth,
With me to Greece and home, or else lie here
Dead at thy side.—But mark me: if thou fear
Lest Artemis be wroth, how can that be?
Hath not her brother's self commanded me
To bear to Greece her image?—Oh, he knew
Her will! He knew that in this land we two
Must meet once more. All that so far hath past
Doth show his work. He will not at the last
Fail. We shall yet see Argos, thou and I.

IPHIGENIA.
To steal for thee the image, yet not die
Myself! 'Tis that we need. 'Tis that doth kill
My hope. Else ... Oh, God knows I have the will!

ORESTES.
How if we slew your savage king?

IPHIGENIA.
                    Ah, no:
He sheltered me, a stranger.

ORESTES.
                    Even so,
If it bring life for me and thee, the deed
May well be dared.

IPHIGENIA.
                    I could not ... Nay; indeed
I thank thee for thy daring.

ORESTES.
                    Canst thou hide
My body in the shrine?

IPHIGENIA.
                    There to abide
Till nightfall, and escape?

ORESTES.
                    Even so; the night
Is the safe time for robbers, as the light
For just men.

IPHIGENIA.
                    There be sacred watchers there
Who needs must see us.

ORESTES.
                    Gods above! What prayer
Can help us then?

IPHIGENIA.
> I think I dimly see
One chance.

ORESTES.
> What chance? Speak out thy fantasy.

IPHIGENIA'.
On thine affliction I would build my way.

ORESTES.
Women have strange devices.

IPHIGENIA.
> I would say
Thou com'st from Hellas with thy mother's blood
Upon thee.

ORESTES.
> Use my shame, if any good
Will follow.

IPHIGENIA.
> Therefore, an offence most high
It were to slay thee to the goddess!

ORESTES.
> Why?
Though I half guess.

IPHIGENIA.
> Thy body is unclean.—
Oh, I will fill them with the fear of sin!

ORESTES.
What help is that for the Image?

IPHIGENIA.
> I will crave
To cleanse thee in the breaking of the wave.

ORESTES.
That leaves the goddess still inside her shrine,
And'tis for her we sailed.

IPHIGENIA.
                    A touch of thine
Defiled her. She too must be purified.

ORESTES.
Where shall it be? Thou knowest where the tide
Sweeps up in a long channel?

IPHIGENIA.
                    Yes! And where
Your ship, I guess, lies moored.

ORESTES.
                    Whose hand will bear—
Should it be thine?—the image from her throne?

IPHIGENIA.
No hand of man may touch it save mine own.

ORESTES.
And Pylades—what part hath he herein?

IPHIGENIA.
The same as thine. He bears the self-same sin.

ORESTES.
How wilt thou work the plan—hid from the king
Or known?

IPHIGENIA.
        To hide it were a hopeless thing..
Oh, I will face him, make him yield to me.

ORESTES.
Well, fifty oars lie waiting on the sea.

IPHIGENIA.
Aye, there comes thy work, till an end be made.

ORESTES.
Good. It needs only that these women aid
Our secret. Do thou speak with them, and find
Words of persuasion. Power is in the mind
Of woman to wake pity.—For the rest,
God knoweth: may it all end for the best!

IPHIGENIA.
O women, you my comrades, in your eyes
I look to read my fate. In you it lies,
That either I find peace, or be cast down
To nothing, robbed for ever of mine own—
Brother, and home, and sister pricelessly
Beloved.—Are we not women, you and I,
A broken race, to one another true,
And strong in our shared secrets? Help me through
This strait; keep hid the secret of our flight,
And share our peril! Honour shineth bright
On her whose lips are steadfast ... Heaven above!
Three souls, but one in fortune, one in love,
Thou seest us go—is it to death or home?
If home, then surely, surely, there shall come
Part of our joy to thee. I swear, I swear
To aid thee also home ...

[she goes to one after another, and presently kneels embracing the
knees of the LEADER.]

                    I make my prayer
By that right hand; to thee, too, by that dear
Cheek; by thy knees; by all that is not here
Of things beloved, by mother, father, child—
Thou hadst a child!—How say ye? Have ye smiled
Or turned from me? For if ye turn away,
I and my brother are lost things this day.

LEADER.
Be of good heart, sweet mistress. Only go
To happiness. No child of man shall know
From us thy secret. Hear me, Zeus on high!

IPHIGENIA (rising).
God bless you for that word, and fill your eye
With light!—

[turning to ORESTES and PYLADES.]

But now, to work! Go thou, and thou,
In to the deeper shrine. King Thoas now
Should soon be here to question if the price
Be yet paid of the strangers' sacrifice.

[ORESTES and PYLADES go in.]

Thou Holy One, that on the shrouded sand
Of Aulis saved me from a father's hand
Blood-maddened, save me now, and save these twain.
Else shall Apollo's lips, through thy disdain,
Be no more true nor trusted in men's eyes.
Come from the friendless shore, the cruel skies,
Come back: what mak'st thou here, when o'er the sea
A clean and joyous land doth call for thee?

[she follows the men into the temple.]

CHORUS.

[STROPHE I.]

Bird of the sea rocks, of the bursting spray,
    O halcyon bird,
That wheelest crying, crying, on thy way;
Who knoweth grief can read the tale of thee:
One love long lost, one song for ever heard
    And wings that sweep the sea.

Sister, I too beside the sea complain,
    A bird that hath no wing.
Oh, for a kind Greek market-place again,
For Artemis that healeth woman's pain; '
    Here I stand hungering.
Give me the little hill above the sea,

The palm of Delos fringed delicately,
The young sweet laurel and the olive-tree
   Grey-leaved and glimmering;
O Isle of Leto, Isle of pain and love;
The Orbed Water and the spell thereof;
Where still the Swan, minstrel of things to be,
   Doth serve the Muse and sing!

[ANTISTROPHE I.]

Ah, the old tears, the old and blinding tears
   I gave God then,
When my town fell, and noise was in mine ears
Of crashing towers, and forth they guided me
Through spears and lifted oars and angry men
   Out to an unknown sea.
They bought my flesh with gold, and sore afraid
   I came to this dark East
To serve, in thrall to Agamemnon's maid,
This Huntress Artemis, to whom is paid
   The blood of no slain beast;
Yet all is bloody where I dwell, Ah me!
Envying, envying that misery
That through all life hath endured changelessly.
   For hard things borne from birth
Make iron of man's heart, and hurt the less.
'Tis change that paineth; and the bitterness
Of life's decay when joy hath ceased to be
   That makes dark all the earth.

   Behold, [STROPHE 2.]
  Two score and ten there be
  Rowers that row for thee,
And a wild hill air, as if Pan were there,
  Shall sound on the Argive sea,
  Piping to set thee free.

  Or is it the stricken string
  Of Apollo's lyre doth sing

Joyously, as he guideth thee
    To Athens, the land of spring;
    While I wait wearying?

    Oh, the wind and the oar,
    When the great sail swells before,
With sheets astrain, like a horse on the rein;
    And on, through the race and roar,
    She feels for the farther shore.

    Ah me, [ANTISTROPHE 2.]
    To rise upon wings and hold
    Straight on up the steeps of gold
Where the joyous Sun in fire doth run,
    Till the wings should faint and fold
    O'er the house that was mine of old:

    Or watch where the glade below
    With a marriage dance doth glow,
And a child will glide from her mother's side
    Out, out, where the dancers flow:
    As I did, long ago.

    Oh, battles of gold and rare
    Raiment and starred hair,
And bright veils crossed amid tresses tossed
    In a dusk of dancing air!
    O Youth and the days that were!

[enter KING THOAS, with soldiers.]

THOAS.
Where is the warden of this sacred gate,
The Greek woman? Is her work ended yet
With those two strangers? Do their bodies lie
Aflame now in the rock-cleft sanctuary?

LEADER. Here is herself, O King, to give thee word. enter, from the
temple, IPHIGENIA, carrying the image on high.

THOAS.
How, child of Agamemnon! Hast thou stirred
From her eternal base, and to the sun
Bearest in thine own arms, the Holy One?

IPHIGENIA.
Back Lord! No step beyond the pillared way.

THOAS.
But how? Some rule is broken?

IPHIGENIA.
                I unsay
That word. Be all unspoken and unwrought!

THOAS.
What means this greeting strange? Disclose thy thought.

IPHIGENIA.
Unclean the prey was that ye caught, O King.

THOAS.
Who showed thee so? Thine own imagining?

IPHIGENIA.
The Image stirred and shuddered from its seat.

THOAS.
Itself? ... Some shock of earthquake loosened it.

IPHIGENIA.
Itself. And the eyes closed one breathing space.

THOAS.
But why? For those two men's bloodguiltiness?

IPHIGENIA.
That, nothing else. For, Oh, their guilt is sore.

THOAS.
They killed some of my herdsmen on the shore?

IPHIGENIA.
Their sin was brought from home, not gathered here.

THOAS.
What? I must know this.—Make thy story clear.

IPHIGENIA. (she puts the image down and moves nearer to thoas.)
The men have slain their mother.

THOAS.
                    God! And these
Be Greeks!

IPHIGENIA
They both are hunted out of Greece.

THOAS.
For this thou has brought the Image to the sun?

IPHIGENIA.
The fire of heaven can cleanse all malison.

THOAS.
How didst thou first hear of their deed of shame?

IPHIGENIA.
When the Image hid its eyes, I questioned them.

THOAS.
Good. Greece hath taught thee many a subtle art.

IPHIGENIA.
Ah, they too had sweet words to move my heart.

THOAS.
Sweet words? How, did they bring some news of Greece?

IPHIGENIA.
Orestes, my one brother, lives in peace.

THOAS.
Surely! Good news to make thee spare their lives ...

IPHIGENIA.
My father too in Argos lives and thrives.

THOAS.
While thou didst think but of the goddess' laws!

IPHIGENIA.
Do I not hate all Greeks? Have I not cause?

THOAS.
Good cause. But now ... What service should be paid?

IPHIGENIA.
The Law of long years needs must be obeyed.

THOAS.
To work then, with thy sword and handwashing!

IPHIGENIA.
First I must shrive them with some cleansing thing.

THOAS.
What? Running water, or the sea's salt spray?

IPHIGENIA.
The sea doth wash all the world's ills away.

THOAS.
For sure. 'Twill make them cleaner for the knife.

IPHIGENIA.
And my hand, too, cleaner for all my life.

THOAS.
Well, the waves lap close by the temple floor.

IPHIGENIA.
We need a secret place. I must do more.

THOAS.
Some rite unseen? 'Tis well. Go where thou wilt.

IPHIGENIA.
The Image likewise must be purged of guilt.

THOAS.
The stain hath touched it of that mother's blood?

IPHIGENIA.
I durst not move it else, from where it stood.

THOAS.
How good thy godliness and forethought! Aye,
Small wonder all our people holds thee high.

IPHIGENIA.
Dost know then what I fain would have?

THOAS.
'Tis thine to speak and it shall be.

IPHIGENIA.
Put bondage on the strangers both ...

THOAS.
Why bondage? Whither can they flee?

IPHIGENIA.
Put not thy faith in any Greek.

THOAS (to ATTENDANTS).
Ho, men! Some thongs and fetters, go!

IPHIGENIA.
Stay; let them lead the strangers here, outside the shrine ...

THOAS.
It shall be so.

IPHIGENIA.
And lay dark raiment on their heads ...

THOAS.
To veil them, lest the Sun should see.

IPHIGENIA.
And lend me some of thine own spears.

THOAS.
This company shall go with thee.

IPHIGENIA.
Next, send through all the city streets a herald ...

THOAS.
Aye; and what to say?

IPHIGENIA.
That no man living stir abroad.

THOAS.
The stain of blood might cross their way.

IPHIGENIA.
Aye, sin like theirs doth spread contagion.

THOAS (to an ATTENDANT).
Forth, and publish my command ...

IPHIGENIA.
That none stir forth—nor look ...

THOAS.
Nor look.—How well thou carest for the land!

IPHIGENIA.
For one whom I am bound to love.

THOAS.
Indeed, I think thou hat'st me not.

IPHIGENIA. And thou meanwhile, here at the temple, wait, O King, and ...

THOAS.
Wait for what?

IPHIGENIA.
Purge all the shrine with fire.

THOAS.
'Twill all be clean before you come again.

IPHIGENIA. And while the strangers pass thee close, seeking the sea
...

THOAS.
What wouldst thou then?

IPHIGENIA.
Put darkness on thine eyes.

THOAS.
Mine eyes might drink the evil of their crime?

IPHIGENIA.

And, should I seem to stay too long ...

THOAS.
Too long? How shall I judge the time?

IPHIGENIA.
Be not dismayed.

THOAS.
Perform thy rite all duly. We have time to spare.

IPHIGENIA.
And God but grant this cleansing end as I desire!

THOAS.
I join thy prayer.

IPHIGENIA. The door doth open! See, they lead the strangers from the cell within, And raiment holy and young lambs, whose blood shall shrive the blood of Sin. And, lo, the light of sacred fires, and things of secret power, arrayed By mine own hand to cleanse aright the strangers, to cleanse Leto's Maid.

[she takes up the image again.]

There passeth here a holy thing: begone, I charge ye,
    from the road,
O whoso by these sacred gates may dwell, hand-consecrate
    to God,
What man hath marriage in his heart, what woman
    goeth great with child,
Begone and tremble from this road: fly swiftly, lest ye
    be defiled.—

O Queen and Virgin, Leto-born, have pity! Let me
    cleanse this stain,
And pray to thee where pray I would: a clean house
    shall be thine again,
And we at last win happiness.—Behold, I speak but as
    I dare;
The rest … Oh, God is wise, and thou, my Mistress,
    thou canst read my prayer.

[The procession passes out, THOAS and the bystanders veiled;
Attendants in front, then IPHIGENIA with the Image, then veiled
Soldiers, then ORESTES and PYLADES bound, the bonds held by
other veiled Soldiers following them. THOAS goes into the Temple.]

CHORUS. [STROPHE.]
  Oh, fair the fruits of Leto blow:
  A Virgin, one, with joyous bow,
  And one a Lord of flashing locks,
    Wise in the harp, Apollo:
  She bore them amid Delian rocks,
    Hid in a fruited hollow.

  But forth she fared from that low reef,
  Sea-cradle of her joy and grief.
  A crag she knew more near the skies
    And lit with wilder water,
  That leaps with joy of Dionyse:
    There brought she son and daughter.

And there, behold, an ancient Snake,
Wine-eyed, bronze-gleaming in the brake
Of deep-leaved laurel, ruled the dell,
  Sent by old Earth from under
Strange caves to guard her oracle—
  A thing of fear and wonder.

Thou, Phoebus, still a new-born thing,
  Meet in thy mother's arms to lie,
Didst kill the Snake and crown thee king,
  In Pytho's land of prophecy:
Thine was the tripod and the chair
Of golden truth; and throned there,
Hard by the streams of Castaly,
  Beneath the untrodden portal
Of Earth's mid stone there flows from thee
  Wisdom for all things mortal.

[ANTISTROPHE.]

He slew the Snake; he cast, men say,
Themis, the child of Earth, away
From Pytho and her hallowed stream;
  Then Earth, in dark derision,
Brought forth the Peoples of the Dream
  And all the tribes of Vision.

And men besought them; and from deep
Confused underworlds of sleep
They showed blind things that erst had been
  And are and yet shall follow
So did avenge that old Earth Queen
  Her child's wrong on Apollo.

Then swiftly flew that conquering one
To Zeus on high, and round the throne
Twining a small indignant hand,
  Prayed him to send redeeming
To Pytho from that troublous band
  Sprung from the darks of dreaming.

Zeus laughed to see the babe, I trow,
So swift to claim his golden rite;
He laughed and bowed his head, in vow
To still those voices of the night.
And so from out the eyes of men
That dark dream-truth was lost again;
And Phoebus, throneed where the throng
  Prays at the golden portal,
Again doth shed in sunlit song
  Hope unto all things mortal.

[enter a MESSENGER, running.]

MESSENGER.
Ho, watchers of the fane! Ho, altar-guard,
Where is King Thoas gone? Undo the barred
Portals, and call the King! The King I seek.

LEADER.
What tidings—if unbidden I may speak?

MESSENGER.
The strangers both are gone, and we beguiled,
By some dark plot of Agamemnon's child:
Fled from the land! And on a barque of Greece
They bear the heaven-sent shape of Artemis.

LEADER.
Thy tale is past belief.—Go, swiftly on,
And find the King. He is but newly gone.

MESSENGER.
Where went he? He must know of what has passed!

LEADER.
I know not where he went. But follow fast
And seek him. Thou wilt light on him ere long.

MESSENGER.
See there! The treason of a woman's tongue!
Ye all are in the plot, I warrant ye!

LEADER.
Thy words are mad! What are the men to me? ...
Go to the palace, go!

MESSENGER (seeing the great knocker on the
        temple door.)
I will not stir
Till word be come by this good messenger
If Thoas be within these gates or no.—

[thundering at the door.]

Ho, loose the portals! Ye within! What ho!
Open, and tell our master one doth stand
Without here, with strange evil in his hand.

[enter THAOS from the temple.]

THOAS.
Who dares before this portal consecrate
Make uproar and lewd battering of the gate?
Thy noise hath broke the Altar's ancient peace.

MESSENGER.
Ye Gods! They swore to me—and bade me cease
My search—the King was gone. And all the while ...!

THOAS.
These women? How? What sought they by such guile?

MESSENGER.
Of them hereafter!—Give me first thine ear
For greater things. The virgin minister
That served our altar, she hath fled from this
And stolen the dread Shape of Artemis,
With those two Greeks. The cleansing was a lie.

THOAS.
She fled?—What wild hope whispered her to fly?

MESSENGER.
The hope to save Orestes. Wonder on!

THOAS.
Orestes—how? Not Clytemnestra's son?

MESSENGER.
And our pledged altar-offering. 'Tis the same.

THOAS.
O marvel beyond marvel! By what name
More rich in wonder can I name thee right?

MESSENGER.
Give not thy mind to that. Let ear and sight
Be mine awhile; and when thou hast heard the whole
Devise how best to trap them ere the goal.

THOAS.
Aye, tell thy tale. Our Tauric seas stretch far,
Where no man may escape my wand of war.

MESSENGER.
Soon as we reached that headland of the sea,
Whereby Orestes' barque lay secretly,
We soldiers holding, by thine own commands,
The chain that bound the strangers, in our hands,
There Agamemnon's daughter made a sign,
Bidding us wait far off, for some divine
And secret fire of cleansing she must make.
We could but do her will. We saw her take
The chain in her own hands and walk behind.
Indeed thy servants bore a troubled mind,
O King, but how do else? So time went by.
Meanwhile to make it seem she wrought some high
Magic, she cried aloud: then came the long
Drone of some strange and necromantic song,
As though she toiled to cleanse that blood; and there

Sat we, that long time, waiting. Till a fear
O'ertook us, that the men might slip their chain
And strike the priestess down and plunge amain
For safety: yet the dread our eyes to fill
With sights unbidden held us, and we still
Sat silent. But at last all spoke as one,
Forbid or not forbid, to hasten on
And find them. On we went, and suddenly,
With oarage poised, like wings upon the sea,
An Argive ship we saw, her fifty men
All benched, and on the shore, with every chain
Cast off, our strangers, standing by the stern!
The prow was held by stay-poles: turn by turn
The anchor-cable rose; some men had strung
Long ropes into a ladder, which they swung
Over the side for those two Greeks to climb.

The plot was open, and we lost no time
But flew to seize the cables and the maid,
And through the stern dragged out the steering-blade,
To spoil her course, and shouted: "Ho, what way
Is this, to sail the seas and steal away
An holy image and its minister?
What man art them, and what man's son, to bear
Our priestess from the land?" And clear thereon
He spoke: "Orestes, Agamemnon's son,
And brother to this maid, whom here in peace
I bear, my long lost sister, back to Greece."

We none the less clung fast to her, and strove
To drag her to thy judgment-seat. Thereof
Came trouble and bruised jaws. For neither they
Nor we had weapons with us. But the way
Hard-beaten fist and heel from those two men
Rained upon ribs and flank—again, again...
To touch was to fall gasping! Aye, they laid
Their mark on all of us, till back we fled
With bleeding crowns, and some with blinded eyes,
Up a rough bank of rock. There on the rise
We found good stones and stood, and fought again.

But archers then came out, and sent a rain
Of arrows from the poop, and drove us back.
And just then—for a wave came, long and black,
And swept them shoreward—lest the priestess' gown
Should feel the sea, Orestes stooping down
Caught her on his left shoulder: then one stride
Out through the sea, the ladder at the side
Was caught, and there amid the benches stood
The maid of Argos and the carven wood
Of heaven, the image of God's daughter high.

And up from the mid galley rose a cry:
"For Greece! For Greece, O children of the shores
Of storm! Give way, and let her feel your oars;
Churn the long waves to foam. The prize is won.
The prize we followed, on and ever on,
Friendless beyond the blue Symplegades."
A roar of glad throats echoed down the breeze
And fifty oars struck, and away she flew.
And while the shelter lasted, she ran true
Full for the harbour-mouth; but ere she well
Reached it, the weather caught her, and the swell
Was strong. Then sudden in her teeth a squall
Drove the sail bellying back. The men withal
Worked with set teeth, kicking against the stream.
But back, still back, striving as in a dream,
She drifted. Then the damsel rose and prayed:
"O Child of Leto, save thy chosen maid
From this dark land to Hellas, and forgive
My theft this day, and let these brave men live.
Dost thou not love thy brother, Holy One?
What marvel if I also love mine own?"

The sailors cried a paean to her prayers,
And set those brown and naked arms of theirs,
Half-mad with strain, quick swinging chime on chime
To the helmsman's shout. But vainly; all the time
Nearer and nearer rockward they were pressed.
One of our men was wading to his breast,
Some others roping a great grappling-hook,

While I sped hot-foot to the town, to look
For thee, my Prince, and tell thee what doth pass.

Come with me, Lord. Bring manacles of brass
And bitter bonds. For now, unless the wave
Fall sudden calm, no mortal power can save
Orestes. There is One that rules the sea
Who grieved for Troy and hates her enemy:
Poseidon's self will give into thine hand
And ours this dog, this troubler of the land—
The priestess, too, who, recking not what blood
Ran red in Aulis, hath betrayed her god!

LEADER.
Woe, woe! To fall in these men's hands again,
Mistress, and die, and see thy brother slain!

THOAS.
Ho, all ye dwellers of my savage town
Set saddle on your steeds, and gallop down
To watch the heads, and gather what is cast
Alive from this Greek wreck. We shall make fast,
By God's help, the blasphemers.—Send a corps
Out in good boats a furlong from the shore;
So we shall either snare them on the seas
Or ride them down by land, and at our ease
Fling them down gulfs of rock, or pale them high
On stakes in the sun, to feed our birds and die.

Women: you knew this plot. Each one of you
Shall know, before the work I have to do
Is done, what torment is.—Enough. A clear
Task is afoot. I must not linger here.

[While THOAS is moving off, his men shouting and running before
and behind him, there comes a sudden blasting light and thunder- roll,
and ATHENA is seen in the air confronting them.]

ATHENA.
Ho, whither now, so hot upon the prey,
King Thoas? It is I that bid thee stay,

Athena, child of Zeus. Turn back this flood
Of wrathful men, and get thee temperate blood.
  Apollo's word and Fate's ordained path
Have led Orestes here, to escape the wrath
Of Them that Hate. To Argos he must bring
His sister's life, and guide that Holy Thing
Which fell from heaven, in mine own land to dwell.
So shall his pain have rest, and all be well.
Thou hast heard my speech, O King. No death from thee
May share Orestes between rocks and sea:
Poseidon for my love doth make the sore
Waves gentle, and set free his labouring oar.

  And thou, O far away—for, far or near
A goddess speaketh and thy heart must hear—
Go on thy ways, Orestes, bearing home
The Image and thy sister. When ye come
To god-built Athens, lo, a land there is
Half hid on Attica's last boundaries,
A little land, hard by Karystus' Rock,
But sacred. It is called by Attic folk
Halae. Build there a temple, and bestow
Therein thine Image, that the world may know
The tale of Tauris and of thee, cast out
From pole to pole of Greece, a blood-hound rout
Of ill thoughts driving thee. So through the whole
Of time to Artemis the Tauropole
Shall men make hymns at Halae. And withal
Give them this law. At each high festival,
A sword, in record of thy death undone,
Shall touch a man's throat, and the red blood run—
One drop, for old religion's sake. In this
Shall live that old red rite of Artemis.
And them, Iphigenia, by the stair
Of Brauron in the rocks, the Key shalt bear
Of Artemis. There shalt thou live and die,
And there have burial. And a gift shall lie
Above thy shrine, fair raiment undefiled
Left upon earth by mothers dead with child.

Ye last, O exiled women, true of heart
And faithful found, ye shall in peace depart,
Each to her home: behold Athena's will.

Orestes, long ago on Ares' Hill
I saved thee, when the votes of Death and Life
Lay equal: and henceforth, when men at strife
So stand, mid equal votes of Life and Death,
My law shall hold that Mercy conquereth.
Begone. Lead forth thy sister from this shore
In peace; and thou, Thoas, be wroth no more.

THOAS.
Most high Athena, he who bows not low
His head to God's word spoken, I scarce know
How such an one doth live. Orestes hath
Fled with mine Image hence ... I bear no wrath.
Nor yet against his sister. There is naught,
Methinks, of honour in a battle fought
'Gainst gods. The strength is theirs. Let those two fare
Forth to thy land and plant mine Image there.
I wish them well.

     These bondwomen no less
I will send free to Greece and happiness,
And stay my galleys' oars, and bid this brand
Be sheathed again, Goddess, at thy command.

ATHENA.
'Tis well, O King. For that which needs must be
Holdeth the high gods as it holdeth thee.

Winds of the north, O winds that laugh and run,
Bear now to Athens Agamemnon's son:
Myself am with you, o'er long leagues of foam
Guiding my sister's hallowed Image home.

[she floats away.]

CHORUS. SOME WOMEN.

Go forth in bliss, O ye whose lot
God shieldeth, that ye perish not!

OTHERS.

O great in our dull world of clay,
  And great in heaven's undying gleam,
Pallas, thy bidding we obey:
And bless thee, for mine ears have heard
The joy and wonder of a word
  Beyond my dream, beyond my dream.

Printed in Great Britain
by Amazon

77112447R00041